Play Yoga

This book is dedicated to the youngest,
to their great capacity of "being":
my everyday commitment is to help
them preserving this capacity for
as long as they can.

SWAMI PRAGYA CHAKSU SARASWATI

CONTENTS

Concept and texts by
LORENA V. PAJALUNGA

Illustrations by
ANNA LÁNG

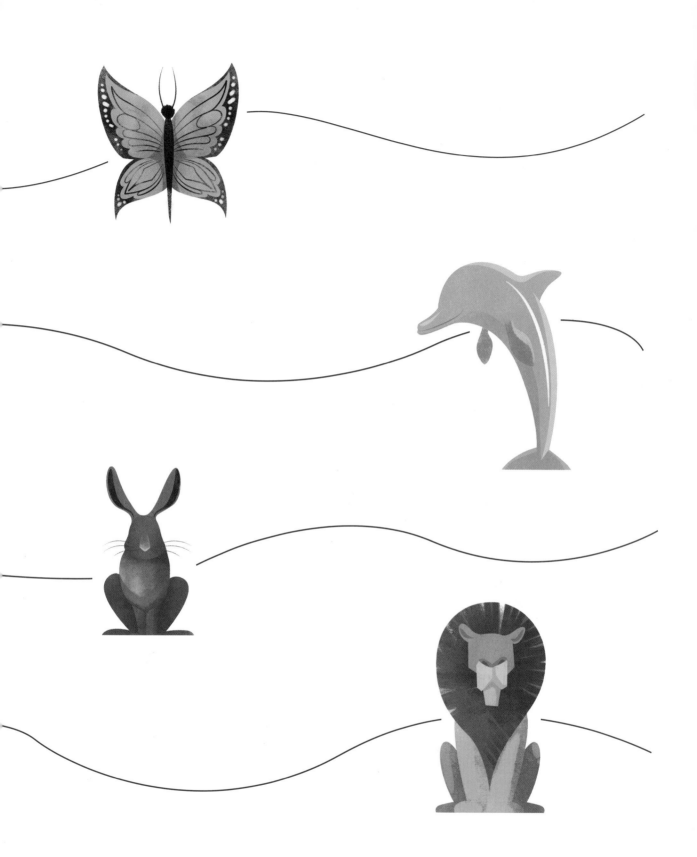

The PLAY YOGA Method

In 1968, Swami Satyananda wrote the book "Yoga for education".

More than thirty years have passed since Satyananda, my teacher in India, gave me a task that, at the time, seemed to be far away from my interests, inclinations and passions.

However, what I myself experienced made me foresee the cross-cultural and educational potential of yoga in its more traditional meaning: so, consistently, I dedicated my whole life to finding out the connections and the points of convergence between East and West of this pedagogical tradition that seemingly is so distant from ours.

The direct contact with children makes me understand, every day, that what they grasp from practice is to be found in a more ancient language, which has its roots in a symbolic level, where words become superfluous.

When you ask a child to become as strong as a lion, or to feel the energy of an eagle, he easily and immediately becomes that energy and that animal. Otherwise, for us adults this process requires a commitment that unravels in a very long route, which passes through mind and reasoning. The result that we obtain can't even be compared to the children's.

This book is dedicated to the youngest, to their great capacity of "being": my everyday commitment is to help them preserving this capacity for as long as they can.

I dedicate this book to all the children in the world, without distinction, with the hope that they can internalize what is proposed to them, and thanking in the meanwhile the adults which I hope will be increasingly aware that a child to play and be happy doesn't need much more than love and "quality presence".

When talking about classical yoga, thoughts run immediately to the yoga proposed by Patanjali, whose journey begins from YAMA and NIYAMA, which constitute universal ethical codes, trans-cultural and multi-religious.

The most beautiful ones are those that lead to non-violence, to respect for oneself and for others, to the art of contentment, to non-attachment, essentially to the study of oneself.

The conscious acquisition of these principles and values allows the practitioner to dedicate himself to the *asanas* (the poses), which must be held for long periods and without effort. Gradually, we will feel that this physical immobility will result also simultaneously in stillness of the mind. Then we will face breathing, concentration practices, control of the senses, meditation.

It is a process, a methodology. In this context, YOGA FOR KIDS has detailed rules and objectives that are exquisitely educational compared to the adult yoga: sometimes the latter erroneously interprets the yogic tradition posing as a search for motion which can appear an end in itself.

In contrast, adults who will try yoga with their children will have to keep in mind that for them it is "the yoga game" and that it must remain this: the *asanas*, the poses in stillness, shouldn't be maintained for a long time.

In fact they are contraindicated and, anyway, children are not able to stay still. So let's respect their wonderful bodies in constant growth and transformation and let's "play" inventing stories with these characters, with their funny poses and absorbing this ancient "knowledge", comforted in this also by studies specifically dedicated to the modern pedagogy.

Spontaneous play stimulates resilience and emotional growth, as the children pour into the fantasy stories all their affection. The characters they encounter become real characters, animated by courage, anger . . . getting in touch with these feelings through playful representation means that they can be better known and processed in real life.

Surely, with the passage of time and with a practice that encourages CREATIVITY and IMAGINATION, also immobility will come spontaneously.

THE EAGLE

✳ STAND STARING AT A POINT IN FRONT OF YOU,
MOVE ALL THE WEIGHT OF YOUR BODY ON YOUR LEFT FOOT.
✳ CROSS THE OTHER LEG SO THAT THE
RIGHT FOOT IS HOOKED TO THE LEFT CALF.
✳ EXTEND YOUR RIGHT ARM AND CROSS THE LEFT ARM
PASSING IT UNDERNEATH, SO THAT YOUR HANDS MEET
AND FORM THE BEAK OF A MIGHTY EAGLE.
✳ REPEAT ON THE OTHER SIDE.

From the eagle learn how to look at things with a sharp eye

THE ELEPHANT

✳ STANDING AND INHALING, BRING YOUR ARMS UP.

✳ JOIN THE PALMS OF YOUR HANDS EXTENDING BACKWARDS.

✳ EXHALING, FLECT FORWARDS, IMITATING THE TRUNK
OF AN ELEPHANT BUSY DRINKING WATER
BEFORE TAKING A REFRESHING SHOWER!

From the elephant learn to be always elegant

THE SEAGULL

✳ STANDING, WITH YOUR LEGS APART, OPEN YOUR ARMS.

✳ FLEX THE BUST FORWARDS.

✳ YOUR ARMS BECOME WINGS, YOUR HEAD AND YOUR GAZE ARE FACING FORWARDS, FOLLOWING THE DIRECTION OF YOUR FLIGHT.

✳ YOUR BREATH IS LONG AND DEEP.

✳ TRY MAKING THE SOUND OF THE SEAGULL . . . WHAT IS IT?

From the seagull learn to feel free

THE DOLPHIN

✳ ON ALL FOURS, AT THE CENTER OF THE MAT,
BRING YOUR ELBOWS TO THE FLOOR.
✳ WHILE EXHALING DEEPLY, STRETCH YOUR KNEES
AND PUT YOUR FEET DOWN.
✳ IN THE POSE OF THE DOLPHIN,
HEAD AND NECK STAY RELAXED.

From the dolphin learn how to have fun with the minimum requirement

THE TORTOISE

✻ SITTING ON THE FLOOR, WITH YOUR LEGS APART,
EXHALE BRINGING YOUR CHEST TO THE FLOOR,
WHILE YOUR ARMS PASS UNDERNEATH YOUR LEGS.
✻ IN THE FINAL POSE YOU'LL HAVE YOUR FOREHEAD ON THE FLOOR
AND THE ELBOWS UNDER YOUR KNEES.
✻ YOU'LL FEEL PROTECTED AS A TORTOISE IN ITS SHELL.

From the tortoise learn wise men's slowness

THE LION

✳ SITTING ON YOUR HEELS, WITH YOUR HANDS TOUCHING YOUR KNEES
AND WITH YOUR EYES SHUT, INHALE DEEPLY AND LIFT YOUR SHOULDERS A BIT,
MAINTAINING YOUR ARMS TENSE.
✳ WHEN YOU EXHALE, YOU FEEL LIKE A VERY ANGRY LION.
OPEN YOUR EYES AND YOUR MOUTH WIDE, STICK YOUR TONGUE OUT
AS MUCH AS YOU CAN, ROARING LOUDLY.
✳ OPEN YOUR FINGERS AS IF THEY WERE THE PAWS OF THE LION
AND PLACE THEM NEXT TO YOUR KNEES, BRINGING ALSO YOUR CHEST FORWARDS.
✳ AFTER THE ROAR, RELAX ONCE AGAIN
AND RETURN TO THE FIRST POSE WITH YOUR EYES SHUT.
✳ ROAR THREE TIMES!

From the lion learn how to be brave in your actions

THE CAT

✳ START FROM THE TABLE POSE, ON ALL FOURS.

✳ BREATHE IN AND ARCH YOUR BACK: IT LOOKS ALMOST LIKE A SMILE.

✳ EXHALE AND ROUND YOUR BACK:

YOUR GAZE GOES TOWARDS THE BELLY BUTTON.

✳ JUST LIKE THE CAT THAT STRETCHES,

LET'S REPEAT A FEW TIMES THIS GREAT POSE.

From the cat learn daydreaming

THE DOG

✳ START FROM THE TABLE POSE:
ON ALL FOURS, LOOKING TO THE FLOOR.
✳ EXHALE BRINGING YOUR WEIGHT ON THE ARMS
AND EXTEND YOUR LEGS.
✳ BRING THE PELVIS UPWARDS.
✳ STRETCH YOUR BACK
LIKE THE DOG AFTER A DEEP SLEEP.

From the dog learn trust and true friendship

THE TIGER

✳ START FROM THE CAT POSE: EXHALE AND ARCH
YOUR BACK, BRINGING THE RIGHT KNEE
TO TOUCH YOUR FOREHEAD.
✳ BREATHE IN AND VIGOROUSLY
BRING BACKWARDS YOUR RIGHT LEG
AS YOU LOOK UPWARDS, AS IF YOU WANTED TO LOOK
AT A FOREST SURROUNDING YOU.
✳ TRY ROARING LIKE A TIGER.
✳ REPEAT ON THE OTHER SIDE.

From the tiger learn fierceness

THE CROCODILE

✳ LIE FACE DOWN WITH YOUR FEET APART
AND THE TOES FACING OUTWARDS.
✳ LEAN YOUR FOREHEAD ON YOUR OVERLAPPING HANDS.
LISTEN TO YOUR BREATH, STAYING STILL.
✳ THIS POSE IS USED IN YOGA FOR RELAXING:
IT'S VERY PLEASANT TO FEEL THE TUMMY
THAT GOES UP AND DOWN IN A NICE MASSAGE.

From the crocodile learn to be very relaxed

THE YAK

❋ PUT YOUR HANDS AT YOUR SIDES,
BRING FORWARDS YOUR RIGHT LEG.
❋ BEND YOUR KNEE.
❋ EXHALE AND ROTATE THE CHEST.
❋ FLEX, BRINGING THE LEFT SHOULDER
NEAR TO THE OPPOSITE KNEE.
❋ RETURN AND REPEAT ON THE OTHER SIDE,
STORING AN INCREDIBLE AMOUNT OF ENERGY.

From the yak learn how to adapt

THE FISH

✳ LIE FACE UP.

✳ BRING YOUR HANDS UNDER
THE GLUTES, WITH DOWNWARDS PALMS.

✳ POINT YOUR ELBOWS TO THE FLOOR AND ARCH YOUR BACK,
DETACHING IT FROM THE FLOOR BREATH AFTER BREATH.

✳ FEEL HEART REGION OPENING
UNTIL YOU HAVE ON THE FLOOR THE TOP OF THE HEAD.

✳ HOW IS THE WORLD FROM UPSIDE DOWN?

From the fish learn to go with the flow

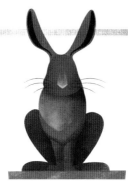

THE HARE

✳ SITTING ON YOUR HEELS, WITH THE FOREHEAD LEANING
ON THE MAT, INTERTWINE YOUR FINGERS
BEHIND YOUR BACK.
✳ EXHALING, DETACH
THE PELVIS FROM THE HEELS.
✳ BRING YOUR HANDS TOWARDS THE SKY.
✳ LEAN ON THE FLOOR THE TOP OF THE HEAD.

From the hare learn quickness

THE LOCUST

✳ LYING FACE DOWN, LEAN YOUR CHIN ON THE MAT.
✳ CLOSE YOUR HANDS IN A FIST,
WITH YOUR THUMBS TUCKED IN.
✳ KEEP YOUR ARMS TENSE UNDER YOUR TORSO.
✳ ACTIVATE YOUR BACK MUSCLES, AND WHILE EXHALING DEEPLY,
RAISE YOUR LEGS UPWARDS AS MUCH AS YOU CAN.

From the locust learn to gather your energy for a great event

THE COBRA

✳ LIE FACE DOWN.

✳ BRING YOUR HANDS UNDER YOUR SHOULDERS
WITH YOUR FINGERS FACING FORWARDS.

✳ EXHALE USING THE STRENGTH OF YOUR ARMS
TO LIFT THE TORSO, JUST LIKE THE COBRA
WHEN IT RISES ABOVE THE OTHER SNAKES.

From the cobra learn majesty

THE BUTTERFLY

✳ SIT ON THE FLOOR,
GET THE SOLES OF YOUR FEET CLOSE
AND SPREAD YOUR HIPS.
✳ GRAB YOUR TOES WITH YOUR HANDS
AND LET YOUR LEGS BOUNCE . . .
✳ IT GENERATES A FLAPPING OF WINGS
THAT MAKES YOU FEEL AS IF YOU COULD
ALMOST LIFT OFF THE FLOOR!

From the butterfly learn the art of lightness

Lorena V. Pajalunga

Lorena V. Pajalunga (Swami Pragya Chaksu Saraswati) thirty years ago has been entrusted by her Master Swami Satyananda of Bihar School of Yoga of Munger, in India, with the task of teaching yoga to children. Thus, she founded the Associazione Italiana Yoga per Bambini (AIYB), that has become a first-level professional master's program provided by the Faculty of Educational Sciences, Università degli Studi Suor Orsola Benincasa, in Naples. With a degree in Human Sciences for Education, she teaches yoga at the GiocaYoga® laboratory at the Department of Pedagogy of the Body of the Bicocca University in Milan.

Anna Láng

Anna Láng is a Hungarian graphic designer and illustrator who currently lives and works in Milan. In Budapest, she attended the University of Fine Arts of Hungary and graduated as graphic designer in 2011. Then she worked for three years in an advertising agency and at the same time she collaborated with the National Theatre of Budapest. In 2013 she won the prize of the city of Békéscsaba at the Hungarian Biennial of Graphic Design with the Shakespeare Posters Series. She currently devotes herself, with great passion, to children illustration.

WHITE STAR KIDS

White Star Kids® is a registered trademark property of White Star s.r.l.

© 2017 White Star s.r.l.
Piazzale Luigi Cadorna, 6 - 20123 Milan, Italy
www.whitestar.it

Translation: Iceigeo, Milan

ISBN 978-88-544-1111-1
1 2 3 4 5 6   21 20 19 18 17

Printed in China

Graphic design by Valentina Figus